Copyright Notice

MW00877309

First Printing, 2013
ISBN-13: 978-1484973431
ISBN-10: 1484973437

Printed in the United States of America

TABLE OF CONTENTS

INTRODUCTION

Thanks for taking the time to look at my book. I appreciate it, and believe it will really help you get the women you desire in the club and bar environment. This book is currently the only one specifically targeting pick-up in the club and bar scene.

It doesn't matter if you're a beginner and are just learning how to pick up women, or you're a seasoned womaniser Casanova type because this book caters for everyone regardless of experience, age or anything else.

You might be wondering 'Who the hell is this guy?' and 'Why should I listen to him?' My living room wall is not adorned with a gold-framed certificate qualifying me in the art of picking up women. Nor do I have a University degree in the art of seduction. What I have written about is purely based upon my own experience and that of others within the pick-up community. Basic psychological techniques that will allow you to create strong bonds and levels of attraction with women that 95% of men will not be able to do.

I was a complete loser with women when I was a kid. I was very shy and socially awkward. I had no female friends and my only experience talking to girls at school was if one asked to borrow a pencil or something. As I went through my teens it got worse and worse, I asked a girl out when I was 14 and was rejected and that just crushed me. Those years were a period of immense frustration and upset.

I hoped that when I was old enough to go to clubs and bars then the situation would change, and I'd be able to play catch up and things would sort themselves out and take their natural course.

When I was 17 I started clubbing with my mates and although I managed to get my first kiss I'd usually end up walking home alone after another fruitless, empty experience feeling depressed and with an empty wallet. I enjoyed getting a kebab though. Earlier I'd spend ages getting ready, doing my hair, wearing nice clothes, but I'd get nothing. Over the next few years I got small bits of sporadic 'success' but it all felt like I'd just been lucky and it was pretty random with girls I didn't necessarily fancy. I was pleased with myself for a bit then I'd realise that in most cases I didn't like them and I was just trying to get my 'number' up.

Things would change when I stumbled across Neil Strauss' 'The Game' a book about a secret community of men who used special techniques and routines to pick up women. It was an eye-opener to say the least. It opened my mind to a whole new world. I realised that success wasn't down to good-looks or money. I used to automatically think that girls would go for my better looking mates, so much so that I didn't even bother trying most of the time. I learned that any average guy can get fantastic results if they followed certain guidelines and advice to help them connect with and ultimately seduce attractive women.

After I read 'The Game' and absorbed it's wisdom I started immersing myself more in the pick-up community and my results improved dramatically. I was getting loads of women. From 2006 onwards I was going out a few times a week and I would get girls numbers, kisses and even sex regularly and quite easily. And I'm not talking average women. I was bedding the kind of girls that most other guys would crawl over hot coals to get with.

I realised all the mistakes I used to make and kicked myself for making them and not making any changes. It's very easy to criticise something in hindsight, so at least I can help you guys and prevent you from making the same mistakes I did.

By 2008 I had started coaching men about pick up in the north of England and also Scandinavia where there was a growing demand and interest in the subject. This is the first time I have condensed everything you need to know about pick up in the club and bar into one book.

Enjoy.

WHY NIGHTCLUB AND BAR GAME?

As opposed to day game or gaming amongst your social circle? Because if you go to a large bar or club then there can be potentially hundreds of attractive women to talk to. It's normal and expected for men to approach women in this environment, many women are actively looking to meet nice, charming and attractive guys like yourselves. There's a more sexual vibe at night, and that coupled with the merriment and drinks flowing freely means it's more conducive to picking up women.

If you decide to do day game, or just meet women who are friends of friends, then you're drastically reducing your chances of getting results. In the day you might come across one attractive woman, maybe none. If you rely on your social circle then you are going to be meeting fewer women of high quality and less frequently. You also have to cope with the potential stigma attached to trying to pick up a girl one of your mates is friends with, or has his eye on. If you go to a club or bar there's going to be loads of hot girls and if there isn't you can just go to another venue. Simple.

You can go up to a woman at night, strike up a conversation and be in bed with her half an hour later. It's a quick and dynamic process that can yield extra fast results if you know what you're doing. You can also meet several women in one evening. Even if you don't take them home you can get multiple phone numbers so there's a larger potential of sex with more girls, more dates, or a higher chance of getting in a relationship. Depends what your goals are.

Why not nightclub and bar game?

ENTERING THE CLUB OR BAR

If you're familiar with the venue and go there a lot then I'd suggest going at your usual time. If you haven't been before I'd recommend 10:30-11:00ish. Not only will you have a better chance of avoiding the dreaded queue, but it will afford you ample time to do a little reconnaissance of your surroundings. What I mean by this is taking a logistical look into where it will be easier and more productive to run game. For example I always try and avoid the downstairs at one of my regular haunts Tiger Tiger. It's mainly a big dance room which is submerged into near darkness for the best part, and it's also extremely loud. My wing and I practically have to shout into each other's ears as loud as we can to get the message across, so there's not much scope for verbal pick up.

There is an area downstairs, just outside the dance room. This consists of a walkway into the room and a small area just next to the toilets where people tend to congregate. This is a much better place to approach someone than in the dance room. It's not that noisy, and its better lit. The girls will feel more comfortable being approached in this environment rather than by a darkened figure appearing from the shadows. Most importantly they can actually hear what you're saying without the need for you to scream in their ear.

Another good place we tend to lurk (Hang on that makes us sound really creepy) I mean hang-out, is upstairs, at an auspicious spot which is both next to a bar and the staircase down to the toilets. This is another high-footfall area, which is not too loud and slightly better lit than some areas of the club. It's an ideal choke point for us to hold throughout the night.

The smoking area is another good place to open sets and you don't even have to smoke to reap the benefits of this place. Many people come out just for some fresh air, or to accompany friends who smoke. It's a welcome quiet place where you don't have to compete with the strains of some demonic synthesised music when you're trying to talk to a girl. Even consider carrying a lighter and cigarettes with you. The amount of times women have approached me and asked for a light is immeasurable. Just doing a small thing like that can help get the ball rolling.

My point about finding a decent vantage point is that rather than haphazardly sprinting round the club like some demented sex addict looking for his next victim, it's better to know what places in the club are the most conducive to your chances of pick up. Randomly going round the club looking for sets of women may have its advantages, which I will touch on later; but by and large a decent location is extremely important and will provide a valuable foundation to build your success upon. If you're hurriedly chasing round the club like a dog on heat then girls are going to see you and realise you're just a predator desperately looking for his next snack.

PRE-OPENER REMINDER

Make sure you don't open head-on. Open slightly to the side. Have your body and feet facing away from the girl and only have your face looking towards her. This looks like a temporary position and gives the impression you won't be hanging round for too long. A head-on approach is intimidating and threatening, especially if you're a woman and it's from a male you don't know. Equally having your feet and body facing away means you can make a quick exit should things go awry, otherwise you'd have to deal with the cumbersome and ungraceful move of repositioning your body and then sauntering off if you wanted to eject. Once the interaction is full steam ahead and you've built some level of comfort and are getting a positive response you'll be able to adopt a more close and personal position.

Under no circumstances approach from behind. Even if you're Ryan Gosling or Leonardo Di Caprio. And definitely don't tap them from behind. It's a plain weird and creepy move. If your target is moving then make sure you walk in front of her and then open with the aforementioned method. Never from behind.

Don't forget the three-second rule too. For those of you not versed fully in the PUA lingo the three- second rule means if you do make eye contact with a girl, don't leave it more than three seconds to approach her. Firstly, if you stare at her for any longer than that without approaching it just looks weird and unsettling, and makes you look indecisive and unconfident. Secondly, if you don't approach within this short window then you may over think things, begin to doubt yourself and as soon as that negativity creeps into your psyche then you've lost the advantage. You have to go for it.

THE OPENER

There is a lot of debate amongst PUA trainers and the community in general about openers. But one thing they all have in common is that none are the 'Magic Bullet'. Despite what some websites and trainers may claim, there is no secret line or routine which will work on every girl every time. If you come across a website offering 'Fool proof' magic lines to attract 'Any woman' take it with the pinch of salt it deserves for this is simply false, so don't waste your time and money on it. Sadly there is no magic line, otherwise everyone would be getting laid all the time, and there would be no point in me writing this book!

Right, so you've identified your target, you've approached but hang on...There are 171,476 words in current use according to the Oxford English dictionary, how do you combine and interweave them to have the desired effect? Don't worry, this section will not only teach you about the different types of opener available to you and how you can implement them in a club and bar setting as well as offer you some tried and tested examples you can take with you into the danger zone.

Opinion Opener

The opinion opener is what I feel is the best method if you're just starting out. Even seasoned PUAs I know who have been in the game for years now swear by them. An opinion opener is a pre-planned question you ask a set, making sure you create the impression that it's totally unplanned and organic. The opinion opener is neutral and non-threatening, and if executed correctly can give you a few minutes of material. It's also beneficial because you can initiate one with a group of several women. As we all know, women love to have an opinion; especially if it revolves around a subject they're interested in such as fashion, relationships etc.

Russell Brand Skinny Jeans

Me: Hey, what do you think of guys who wear skinny jeans?

Girl: Yeah I think they're hot etc!

Me: I was thinking about getting some because Russell Brand wears them and he gets all the women. Do you think girls like him because of what he wears or because he's rich and famous?

Girl: I don't like him but I think because he's rich and famous. Etc etc.

Me: Well that shows me how shallow women are. Can't believe you don't like Russell Brand.

Girl: He's just a slag and he's too hairy etc etc

Me: Yeah right, if you came home tonight and he was in your bed completely naked you wouldn't tell him to leave I bet.

Girl: Haha maybe not then.

I then might transition into an abstract but light comical routine

Me: Yeah and then you could sleep with him and then sell the story to 'The Sun'

Girl: Haha

Me: But it was my idea so I get 75 percent of the money.

If the girl says she like Russell brand you could say you like his show 'Ponderland' or remind her of some of his best jokes. You've unearthed some common ground and can go from there.

When's the right time to text?

Your mate went on a date with a girl he really likes earlier this evening. He thinks she really likes him too and wants to text her to say he wants to see her again but doesn't want to appear needy and overly keen. How long should he leave to text her? You think that evening, but another friend thinks the next day? Most women as I said love to talk about relationships and would be happy to impart their worldy knowledge.

Do I look like a drug dealer?

I attribute this opener to the legendary Cajun. If you're wearing a leather jacket just ask the set if they think you look like a drug dealer. Then say you've had three people asking you for drugs and you don't know if it's anything to do with the leather jacket.

Does this shirt make me look Gay?

You approach and ask if your shirt makes you look gay. An effective opener I have used whilst sporting a pink shirt. I've used this with a lot of success before. Women like to talk fashion and the unthreatening nature can easily integrate you into a set. You could then transition into how you don't have a 'Gaydar' and wonder how some people do.

Do you believe in Psychics?

Psychics, tarot cards and palm readings are another topic women are interested in. Loads of women like this stuff and its possible they've even been to see one or know someone who has. You could even say your mate is a psychic and that you didn't used to believe in it but some of the things he can do have convinced you. Don't say that you have psychic abilities and you can see yourself in bed with them come the end of the night.

Situational opener

You have to ad-Lib a little here because it involves observing something in the microcosm of what you can see and commenting on it in an interesting and if possible amusing manner.

Have you seen that guy's shirt?

That girl's a great dancer

How long does it take to get served in here?

Don't you just hate guys that wear trainers in clubs?

Why is that guy sat in the corner listening to an IPod?

These openers allow you to go under the radar with the girl. They're non-threatening and give the impression you're simply making an observation rather than trying to chat them up. A situational opener negates the need to learn and remember a routine because you can just instinctively look around for inspiration and make something up on the spot from the myriad of human interactions and quirks you witness.

Indirect opener

Hey it's you again!

Feign knowing a girl, but do it with charm and conviction so that she's not sure she hasn't met you on a night out before. If she says where do you know her from just name a few popular local bars or clubs and say you bumped into her there once.

Are you copying her style?

Point to a woman in the vicinity who's wearing an outfit resembling what the target has on and ask if she's copying said girl's style. The target should quickly try and validate herself by denying it and then you can tease her.

Who's the biggest player out of you lot?

Absurd opener delivered with a straight, genuine face. If they point to a particular girl you could agree that she looks like a player, or you could say you thought a different member of the set was. Be prepared to give a reason if they ask you why.

Have you seen Kieron?

Or John, Paul, Chunk, it's irrelevant. Ask if they've seen your fictional friend and inevitably when they say no you ask them if they're sure and then describe 'him'. You could then say to the girl that she looks similar to or has the same outfit on as Kieron's female friend Helen, Or Laura or whatever, doesn't matter because she doesn't exist. Don't feel guilty about lying, it's an indirect non threatening opener to engage with a one or two set.

Are you guys coming to the after party?

Again so absurd but say Michael Douglas is in town and he has Heinz Tomato Soup, Cathedral City cheddar and various other nibbles and he's looking to fill a select VIP list for later. Only an uptight girl wouldn't find this amusing.

If I wasn't gay you'd so be mine

The target won't see you as a threat if you say this allowing you to interact without obstruction. You can later admit you aren't gay and she'll already be so fond of you it won't matter that you were just kidding.

Have we fucked before?

A friend of mine uses this on a regular basis. I don't personally but if you have the balls to do it and if the girl's not uptight she may find it funny. I'd probably make sure there weren't any male friends or hefty female ones around before I used this one.

Can I snog you?

Another risky line and one you have to have balls to use. Some girls might think how brash you are is funny, and then you could joke about that being the worst line she's heard all night. There are better lines than this and I'm not taking the piss including this in the section I'm just trying to demonstrate the wild variety of tools at your disposal and the fact that lines which might sound stupid can actually be applied successfully on a night out.

You have nice eyes can I touch them?

Another surreal opener. Sometimes gets a laugh when I use it.

Is there a room in here which just plays Coldplay?

Should force a laugh or some intrigue, especially if delivered with a confident conviction like it's the most normal thing to ask in the world.

Direct opener

Now when you get a little bit more experienced and confident at opening sets I would suggest experimenting with a direct opener. I cannot reiterate enough that these need to be delivered as strongly and confidently as possible with a loud and clear voice. This should be coupled with assured and sincere eye contact. You must believe in yourself 100 percent when you're imparting these. Practice in the mirror before you go out if you need to, and imagine the way Brad Pitt or Channing Tatum might say them and try and replicate.

If you can master this then it can yield quick results without the need of the traditional more slow paced routines, and you know that if she reacts positively then half the battle is won and you can concentrate on escalating.

On nights out, guys often use direct openers and do not get anywhere because they don't have the confidence and assuredness that you will have. A girl can sense if you're unsure and unconfident so make sure you're the opposite before you lock and load.

Here are a few examples.

You're really sexy what's your name?

You're very beautiful aren't you? (Introduce yourself)

I saw you from over there and thought I'd kick myself later if I didn't say hi.

Can I fuck you? (Just kidding, I wouldn't try this. Maybe if you asked 1000 women then one would say yes)

I've gone through with you the different types of openers. Opinion, Situational, Indirect and Direct. As I said there is no

'Magic bullet' line or routine and each of these varieties has its advantages and disadvantages. It would be dishonest for me to say that one kind of opener was better than another, it simply depends on what you feel comfortable with and what you feel works for you.

Right now I tend to use opinion openers because they give me more time to incorporate humour which is perhaps my biggest attribute during game. Sometimes the precise spot where you are in a club, maybe it's too loud and you see someone you like, but the noise might make it difficult to run a long routine, thusly a quick direct opener could be more beneficial. In a club you have to improvise so make sure you have several examples of each opener in your artillery.

MID-GAME

Congratulations; you've successfully opened which is the hardest part! Most guys in a club or bar will just stand there nursing their pint, staring at the women they desire, praying that by some quirk of fate one is going to approach them and start chatting them up. Women might do this occasionally but as a general rule they won't, but you're intelligent enough to realise this so let's make the transition to mid game.

This is where you show your true colours and differentiate yourself from the rest of the flock by demonstrating your natural conversation skills. A successful mid-game will mean you are ready to move onto the vital stage of closing. This will require you building rapport and connection with the girl, and setting you aside from the other guys. Don't forget that just because you opened well doesn't mean the girl will be fully invested in you just yet, so don't get complacent. You will be expected to still contribute the majority of the conversation until you hit the hook point (Moment when target is fully ingratiated in the interaction) If you put too much of the conversational onus on her before you have reached the hook point then you run the risk of her ejecting from the conversation.

Now some of you might feel daunted. It's one thing building up the courage to use an opener but making interesting conversation with an attractive woman might seem quite intimidating. Don't let this affect you. I assume most of you have families and friends and I'm sure most of them enjoy your conversation and find you funny, interesting and good company. This is because they've known you for a while and you've built a relationship over time.

When you are doing night game you have to bear in mind that you will face logistical and time constraints. A girl might be passing and you only have a few minutes to get her attention, or her friends might be waiting for her and even if she likes you, you still have a limited amount of time to make an impression because her friends are putting pressure on her to go to the bar. What you will learn in the section below is how to build the rapport and connection in a relatively small amount of time so the time constraint doesn't become too much of an obstacle.

Firstly I will mention what you should try and avoid. Many guys, me included before I learnt game would strike up a conversation with a woman and then ask her a series of mundane, boring interview type questions she's probably heard from half a dozen guys that same night. Things like: *How old are you? What do you do for work? What sports do you like? What food do you like? Do you like the food that you like? What's the size of the club in square feet?* If you just fire endless questions at a girl she will soon get bored. You need to differentiate yourself from the other men by asking a question and then connecting and building rapport revolving around that one question. I know a lot of guys just ask loads of questions to fill any pauses and awkward silences, but you will develop conversational skills, and in time become a lot more interesting from a woman's perspective.

I'd also avoid making physical compliments right away. Things like saying she's really pretty or telling her she has beautiful eyes. Girls like compliments but not at this stage. Any hot girl has probably had countless men tell her she's pretty. If you have to compliment her then make a unique observation for example tell her she has nice hands or you like the way her outfit is coordinated with her bag. Something original, not some obsequious form of flattery. The only circumstance when you make an initial physical compliment is with a direct opener as I mentioned earlier.

Hooks

Some of you might be familiar with what a hook is, but for those who aren't a hook is basically anything that a girl says to you. Anything she says and talks about can be something that you pick up on and use as a tool to steer and expand the conversation to a better level of connection. It could be something as simple as a film she mentions or her favourite holiday destination. For example she could say she loves to travel and she's been to New York recently. Now you have two things you can talk to her about and build a conversation around, travelling and New York. You can evolve it and build rapport and use other hooks to build upon these foundations. The best way to work a hook is to follow it positively. The worst thing you can do is be negative or start talking exclusively about yourself. Below I will demonstrate the different ways you can act upon a hook.

Self-Relating Hook

Me: So where are you from?

Her: Madrid

Me: Oh I love Madrid I love going clubbing there and I support Real Madrid, Gonzalo Higuain is my favourite player. Do you like travelling?

Her: Yes, I enjoyed travelling round Australia.

Me: Oh right, I love travelling I loved going on safari in Africa it's amazing.

The self-relating hook is not recommended. It might work occasionally if you have other abilities in your skill set which you can utilise, but when you're just starting out I wouldn't bother. In this scenario I'm creating hooks which is great, but I am not capitalising upon them and building connection with the girl. I'm instead reflecting upon my own subjective experiences and I'm not really getting into her headspace. She is throwing me a line, giving me the opportunity to engage with her but I'm not taking the bait and ergo I'm not building the rapport needed to take things to the next level. This is a common mistake. Some guys who are new and inexperienced just speak without thinking and say the first thing which comes into their head purely to prolong the interaction. You need to be taking advantage of your hooks and building a deeper personal connection.

The Job Interview hook

Me: So how old are you?

Her: 28.

Me: Cool, so where do you work?

Her: Nandi's.

Me: ok, what do you do for fun?

Her: I play the flute.

Me: Do you like it?

Her: It's ok.

Me: What's the GDP of Equatorial Guinea?

Her: Don't know.

As I mentioned earlier this is the job interview interrogation style attempt to connect. Like with the self relating hooks many AFCs use this technique in a desperate effort to gain rapport and to elongate the conversation. It usually won't work unless she's physically attracted to you, and even if she is it will only afford you a little extra time to get your act together. This routine is boring to any woman and just imagine a random person asking you all these questions; I know I wouldn't want to hang around.

The deeper hook

Me: So have you been travelling much?

Her: Yeah I've been all around the world

Me: That doesn't surprise me. You seem like an open minded person who has the spirit of adventure. I think it's really good how you travelled the world. Some people are just content to go lie on a beach and go clubbing in Magaluf once a year. What do you do for a job?

Her: I'm a nurse.

Me: I guess you're a very kind and compassionate as well as caring person. Some people work just to make money but being in nursing shows your altruistic nature and the fact that you like to help people which is awesome. What do you do for fun?

Her: I play the guitar in a band.

Me: I like the fact that you are creative and have a talent. Many people just watch TV but you show you have discipline and dedication in something you really care about. I guess it must be a great feeling being on stage performing to a crowd of screaming fans knowing that you're doing something you're passionate about.

The deeper hook technique is the best method you can use to establish deep connection. The fact that you're demonstrating close interest shows you're understanding her and deepens the conversation very quickly, as opposed to using the inferior job interview and self relating hook systems. It's a very powerful technique because the deeper you go and more understanding you show, the more likely it is that she will open up, and that's where you can really make a deep connection and create the illusion that you've known each other for longer. Doing this unlocks thoughts and feelings so profound they'd normally only be shared with close family and friends. Use of this system can help transcend the relative short time you've known each other if applied correctly.

Indicators of interest

By this stage in the interaction the target is obviously happy to stay and speak to you. If she's attracted to you then there are some tell-tale signs (Indicators of interest) that will tell you this. I know a lot of guys find it hard to pick up on these so I will make them very clear.

She touches her chest as she's talking to you. Usually the biggest sign that she's sexually interested in you.

She comes back from the toilet with reapplied make-up or lip-gloss. She wants to make herself look pretty for you so you should be pulling the trigger soon.

She doesn't show any sign of wanting to get back to her friends or even better her friends have left the club and left you two alone. This is a sign that she's totally at ease with you and she may have made her friends aware she's fine alone with you. You should think about extracting her out the club and back to yours.

She gives you the 'Double-look'. Another obvious sign of sexual attraction. You need to kiss her there and then whilst the attraction level is at it's pinnacle.

She asks if you're gay. This is because she wants to kiss you and you haven't already tried. Again you should kiss her whilst the attraction is at it's apex.

She bumps into you on the dance floor. A simple way to let you know she's interested. Grab her by the waist and if she's comfortable with it then escalate asap.

She mentions your girlfriend, even if you don't have one. She's just trying to find out if you're single.

She keeps touching you. Yes she could be a tactile kind of girl but if the touches are tenderer, lingering ones then she's attracted to you.

She looks at your mouth. Means she wants to kiss you.

She is happy to listen to you talk even if it's not that interesting. If she wasn't attracted to you she might have left but you should go for it before the attraction dissipates.

Some of these next IOIs are weaker ones so I would make sure they were partnered with the above ones before you go for it.

She laughs at your jokes that aren't even funny. A weaker IOI because she could just be nervous with you and laughing to divert the awkward tension away.

She tilts her head whilst talking to you. When girls expose their neck it's a way of feminising themselves and making themselves vulnerable, however it can be a technique to show empathy and understanding towards you. It may or may not be a direct IOI so make sure you couple it with one in the above section before you proceed.

Rapport building questions

Once you have established a great connection you can take this even deeper with rapport building questions. These questions serve to make the girl feel as comfortable as she would with close family and friends, in a very short space of time. I will list some examples you can use.

You are beautiful but so are many girls in here. What puts you aside from all the others?

This is a good challenge and by the rapport building stage the girl should be willing to prove herself to you. You should not use this as an opener because at this stage she probably won't invest in a challenge from a complete stranger. If she says she is caring or lists another nice quality then reward her by saying that yes you got that impression.

What was your favourite TV show as a child? Which TV show is the first you remember watching?

This is a good one to gain an insight into her childhood innocence. Something she ordinarily wouldn't share with someone she just met. It also evokes happy and personal memories which she will relate to you creating. Whatever her answer make sure you're sensitive because although it's only a TV show it may elicit very important memories to her.

Have you ever been in love?

This is a much used question amongst the community because of the emotional power it channels. If she has been don't ask what happened just talk about how wonderful love is and remember talking about the emotions and memories with you will accelerate the connection, and subconsciously she will relate these feelings to your presence.

If you could live one experience of your life again what would it be and why?

Again this is very good at eliciting feelings and emotions because it will make her remember fond and special memories that she will associate with being with you. Again it's a conversation you would only have normally with someone very close so can help you quickly build a deep bond.

What do you remember about your first day at school?

This can create very happy and fond memories, looking back into her childhood and again going into a deeper zone that she would normally only do with a guy after knowing him for several months or possibly not at all.

If you want some more examples then there are dozens online that can be found with a quick Google search or feel free to invent your own. Use which ones you feel work best but for you and be prepared to have an interesting answer if she asks you a question in return.

Isolating the target

You should have built enough connection, rapport and attraction by now to isolate your target which basically means to get her away from her friends to a spot where it's just you two, where you can further escalate and think about closing. I will now teach you how to do this in a seamless and non-creepy fashion.

You need to be decisive and act with utter confidence. Say something like 'Come on let's get a drink' 'Let's go and dance' or 'Come outside with me for a cigarette'. You need to be decisive because decision is a quality of an alpha male. If you've already built a connection there is no reason why your target won't want to go with you.

Sexual Escalation

So you're sat down with your girl. By now you have her undivided attention, but you haven't kissed her, or even given any indication you want to. This is the seduction level where you show the girl you're attracted to her with certain subtle changes to the rhythm and tone of your voice and eye contact. You may also do this by sexualising the conversation.

Many guys find sexual escalation a particular sticking point. I know I certainly did so if you find it hard you're not alone. By this point you might have invested a lot of time in the girl and everything is going swimmingly. You managed to open, negotiate mid-game and have isolated the target. You've overcome considerable obstacles to get in the position you're in, and now you're worried about screwing it up.

Some guys get so worked up about this they don't do anything, the moment is lost and so is the girl. Like I said before you need to be decisive and demonstrate you're an alpha male who makes no apologies for his wants and desires. Don't expect the girl to sexually escalate, this may happen rarely but generally speaking in this dynamic the onus is always on the man.

You need to realise that nothing great is achieved without sacrifice and that you need to sexually escalate because if you don't do it then you'll wake up alone the next day and wish you'd listened to me. I know there's a slight risk involved after all the time and effort you've invested, but not to act on it is weak and befitting of an AFC.

Even if you are planning on sexually escalating, a mistake is simply leaving it too late. If you remain in the deep comfort and rapport phase for too long then you're essentially friends and not potential lovers and she might even think you're gay. A lot of men are also afraid to escalate because they fear they are betraying the girl and being sleazy, rude or creepy. None of these pejoratives are true and if this is what you think you need to internalise that this is simply a form of flirting.

32

So now that's out of the way here are some ways to sexually escalate. This is the moment when you officially begin flirting, build up a bit of excitement, heat and sexual tension. You know you're almost there so you can relax and have some fun. You've already made her comfortable with you but that's not enough to attract her, she's probably comfortable with her male friends as well.

You have to make her feel desirable and sexy in an unapologetic and confident manner. If you're unsure or unconfident then women are more intuitive than men and can detect that. Just internalise the belief that you're the man and when you escalate she is going to like it. You need to act with decision and self belief. Imagine how sexual bad boys like Robbie Williams, Colin Farrell and Kieron Jackson would act and follow suit.

Going back to where I mentioned eye contact was very important in sexual escalation. Just imagine an imaginary triangle on a girls face between her two eyes and nose. You should start by looking at her left eye, then slowly to the right, then slowly down to the lips. This tells her that you find her very attractive and that you want to kiss her there and then. A lot of people in the community I know use this technique with great efficiency.

You can make subtle changes to your voice and the way you speak too. It's more seductive if you slow down the rhythm of your speech. I don't mean to a monotone robotic pace I just mean slightly less so than usual and punctuate words with extra pauses. You also need to decrease the volume of your voice. It doesn't matter exactly what you're talking about, just use common sense, but if you employ this technique then it's a good way to build sexual tension.

Kino-escalation

Kino-escalation refers to touching a girl in small steps, slowly over time making her progressively more comfortable with your touch and proximity.

It might sound intimidating touching a woman if you don't have much experience but you need to grab the bull by the horns and be an alpha male. I will explain the steps you can use to smoothly transition to a kiss.

Light Kino

You must begin with light kino to start off with. This is short and quick kino that almost doesn't register, and she will be comfortable with as it's not too forward. You would concentrate on her hands, arms and shoulders. The touch would be friendly and playful, the way you'd touch a family member or a friend during banter. She will not resist the touch or think it's weird if you keep the touching quick and almost incidental.

Arm touch. Whilst talking lightly brush against her arm with your hand.

Shoulder touch. Lightly touch her shoulder as if you're emphasising something you're saying

High-Five. A good one if you agree on something

Pat on shoulder. Jokingly pat her if she says something stupid or uncool.

Poke on shoulder. Gently poke her and jokingly tell her off or disapprove with something she says.

Short handholding. Tell her she has little hands or something and use it as an excuse to quickly hold her hand.

Jewellery. If she has a ring on use having a look at it as an excuse to touch her hand.

Mid Kino

When you determine she's comfortable with light kino you can move onto mid kino which is still playful, but more intimate. You should now look to touch more private body parts such as her back, waist and knee. Touches in the mid kino stage are often longer and more deliberate but to test the water you should proceed with quick touches on those areas at first to gauge her comfort. Here are some examples you can use.

Hugging. You could hug her as a reward for something cool she's done.

Hand on your leg. Take her hand and put it on your leg.

Hand on her knee. Squeeze it gently mixing up sensual with playful.

Soft touch. Run your fingertips over the back of her hand, her neck or inner arm.

Caress her back. Gently and sensually touch and caress her.

Stomach touch. Find an excuse to touch e.g. she has a flat stomach and gauge how comfortable she is with you touching it.

Hand play. Play with her hand with your fingers.

Heavy Kino

To take this next step use common sense to determine if she's comfortable with the mid kino. Heavy kino is more seductive and intimate still. This would mean concentrating on her neck and facial area. Ears, lips and hair. Again test the waters with quick touches to see if she's comfortable before you continue with longer, lingering ones.

Smelling. You smell her neck or hair and tell her how good she smells.

Hair play. Play with her hair. Any woman who is comfortable with this is attracted to you.

Biting. Gentle biting on her neck.

Sit on lap. Get her to sit on your lap and hold her body.

Massage. Give her a shoulder or hand massage.

Kissing. The final stage of heavy kino.

Remember the first time you kino-escalate at each step you should release it. The withdrawal is what increases the attraction and makes her want more. After she's comfortable with an escalation step she will be more open to longer and more lingering touches.

The psychology of it is that when people are attracted to each other they want to touch each other. Humans like to be touched by people they like. Every time you take an escalation step forward don't forget to calibrate to check if she's comfortable with it.

If you detect she is uncomfortable with escalation then you must release the touch before she resists. If you release then there is nothing to resist from. She is not necessarily rejecting you, she's just saying not yet. If this happens then you can show disinterest as a result of the resistance. You could stop the kino and adopt negative body language. She will feel a sense of loss and know she did something wrong, ergo she will feel like she has to come chase you and make it up. Wait for her to bring something back into the interaction. If she doesn't then slowly start the escalation again. She will be more open to a second attempt because it's more favourable than when you went cold on her.

CLOSING

You're here; the Holy Grail is in your crosshairs. It's time to lock and load gentleman because we're entering the kill zone. In the words of Alec Baldwin in Glengarry Glen Ross 'A-B-C...Always be closing'. To close means to seal the deal in what I class as four ways. Facebook close, N-close (Number close), K-close (Kiss close) and F-close (Fuck close)

Kiss close or Fuck Close are known as 'solid closes' and a simple Facebook close is the weakest type. The most common close you would expect is the number close because it's not always logistically possible to take a girl home there and then at that precise moment.

Number close (N-close)

If you sense that you won't be able to take the girl home then always go for the number rather than begging and trying to convince her to come home with you, unless you want to undo all the hard work you've put in. Say you have to leave and find your friends, thusly giving you the edge and control of the interaction. Make sure you do this at the apex of the engagement, rather than when there's a lull or a decrease in energy or sexual tension. The logic behind this is that it will leave her wanting more and hence you're more likely to hear from her in the future.

Remember girls like decision and confidence so just ask her to put her number in your phone and say you'll give her a text sometime. You could also then ring her phone so she has your number then joke not to get clingy and start ringing you at 6am. What I sometimes do is add a playful element by saving her number under a nickname such as 'Little Laura' or whatever. Having a pet name is something people who have been in a relationship for a while do, so it further adds to the feeling of closeness you share, as well as being a playful gesture.

Kiss close (K-Close)

Many guys find this difficult. They worry about what happens if the girl doesn't want to kiss them and how they'll react to the possible rejection.

If you are able to talk to girls and kiss them then good for you but for those less certain rest assured there are techniques you can employ to smoothly build up for a kiss.

Touch her sensually; her arm, her hand, her hair. If you judge her to be comfortable with you touching her hair then you can go for it.

Hold her hand and squeeze it; if she squeezes back she is ready for a kiss.

At a quiet moment tilt your head slightly and look at her seductively. If she's comfortable with this then it's a green light.

Ask her if she wants to kiss you. Many PUAs including Neil Straus and Mystery advocate this. If she smiles, nods or says yes you know what to do. If she says maybe then that means yes and proceed and if she says no then take a step back and escalate again. Just because she says no verbally doesn't necessarily mean that she actually doesn't want to kiss you.

You can also use the sexual escalation techniques I mentioned earlier including changing your speech pattern, tone and rhythm and the 'Imaginary triangle' eye contact technique.

These are all good methods to escalate to a kiss if you're unsure. You just have to act confidently and go for it!

Fuck Close (F-Close)

Fuck Closes or SNLs (Same night lays) are obviously easier after meeting at a club or bar than after meeting in the day. I tend to go for F-closes on the night but this does not mean I'm not a gentleman or that I treat women badly. I just prefer a casual relationship at the moment plus I have a high sex drive so I prefer to have a constant stream of women in my life, rather than just seeing the same one repeatedly.

I strongly recommend going for SNLs if you're not bothered about the possibility of it just being a one-night stand.

Sometimes you meet a girl and it's just right at that exact moment. Maybe if you met her again somewhere else there might not be a spark or attraction or maybe one of billions of permutations and variables could dictate that it has to happen that night and only that night.

I think they are even conducive for better relationships. If you sleep with someone straight away I believe that you can be at ease with each other faster. I think most of you would admit that you act differently, even slightly after you've slept with a girl. There isn't that tension and nervous energy surrounding you whereby you're scared or anxious you'll do something wrong and screw it up. For me personally I just feel more relaxed after I've had sex with a girl.

That's just me anyway. If you're not looking to just have sex then concentrate on your number closes and deep connections. For the others I will detail some advice to help improve your chances of getting a same night lay.

I've had a lot of SNLs and my experience tells me that a lot of girls are up for sex the night of meeting. You must be aware however, that girl's attitudes towards these do vary.

Some girls are simply drunk and horny or just horny and are just looking for sex. They are very easily persuaded and if you escalate quickly you can take them home very easily. You just need to be proactive and confident and say something like 'Come on let's get out of here' or 'Let's go and get some fresh air' and literally walk them out of the club. More girls are like this than you think. I've boned a girl in a club toilet before.

Had sex with one behind a bin in a city centre as well as having a sex act performed on me in a park on the way home, down an alley and whilst sat on a sofa in a club. This is the kind of fun you can be having with this type of girl.

The next level girl doesn't have one-night stands willy-nilly like the aforementioned girl. This doesn't mean she can't be persuaded. She's not a slut but needs more than just being physically turned on, so make sure you build some strong comfort and a good connection.

The most difficult kind of girl to have a SNL with would not usually consider sleeping with a guy she's just met. It might not have even felt right to try and kiss her yet so don't force it. You will have to create an even more powerful connection and strong bond between the two of you, and make sure you build some sexual tension so there's an attraction, but don't overdo it. If you invite her back to yours or are invited to hers make sure there is no sexual suggestion whatsoever. You should suggest you go somewhere more quiet to talk or where you can show her some funny videos on YouTube for example. When you get home offer her a drink and wait a while until she's comfortable before you try and kiss her. You can try and sexually escalate but if she shows resistance take a step back and escalate again. You will have to move very slowly and take small steps so be patient.

FURTHER WAYS TO IMPROVE YOUR GAME

This section details various techniques and methods you can employ to help you improve at picking up women.

Creating social proof

Social proof is a very important aspect in pick up and can really make life easier if you know how to create it.

If you're in a club people will formulate a superficial impression of you based upon how you engage with certain other people. Just picture this. A girl sees you being the centre of attention, attractive girls chatting to you and laughing at your jokes. Bouncers saying 'Hi' and shaking your hand, and the club promoters and managers hanging onto your every word. This will make a big impression on all the girls that witness it. They are going to think 'This guy must be cool because all these people are talking to him.'

Just think how much better this social proof makes you appear than if you were skulking in a corner low energy nursing your pint not speaking to anyone. Girls want to know the interesting guy who is standing out and having a laugh. Positive social proof is a key element to improving your game and here's how to do it.

1: When you enter the club start saying 'Hi' or 'Cheers' to random people guys and girls. Ask them what their names are, make small talk for a few second then leave. This is better at small venues but it's creating the impression throughout the room that you're Mr Sociable. You didn't outstay your welcome and next time you walk round the room people will recognise you and you can interact again. It won't be as threatening and intimidating to girls if you've already said 'Hi' earlier.

2: If you go to a club on a regular basis get to know the bouncers. Just make friendly small talk in the queue like 'You guys must get so many girls working here' A little ego massaging can go a long way. Introduce yourself, get their name and next time you go they might let you skip the queue. Also if you see them inside you can shake hands creating positive social proof.

3: Most clubs have a promotions team these days so get to know the event manager and the guy who runs guest list. Introduce yourself, get their names and compliment them on how good their night is. If you do this they'll remember you and the more times you see them you might benefit from all sorts of perks like getting queue jump to cheaper drinks and VIP access. It also looks cool if girls see you talking to them inside the club. Talk to the female promoters too, don't run game on them just be normal and friendly and they might approach you in the club increasing your value to other women.

4: Go out with attractive girls. If you go clubbing with an attractive girl then your value will skyrocket. If women see you talking to and making a hot female friend laugh then this is the ultimate social proof. Women will think you must be a cool guy if you're hanging around with hot girls and it makes it a lot easier to run game. Your friend can introduce you to women and the proof she provides means it will be a lot easier to start an interaction than if you were by yourself or with a wing man. Do not underestimate the power of a hot female winging you.

If you incorporate all these steps then you will be creating a lot of intrigue and you'll be proving yourself to be a high value individual. It's basic human psychology that women will be more attracted and drawn to men of value and high social standing.

Dance floor game

You're doing yourself a disservice if you don't utilise the dance floor to get girls. You'll find many hot women on the dance floor. Being able to dance is a good tool to have and a very attractive quality from a woman's perspective. It shows how confident you are, how alpha you are and even how good in bed you are, plus it's great fun once you get into it. You can use it to get a girl away from her friends too.

If you have a bit of spare cash I would recommend paying for dance lessons. It doesn't have to be for very long and it's relatively inexpensive. Lessons are definitely worthwhile to pick up some tips and tricks, so you can look better than the other guys in the club. Just have a look on Google and see what's available in your area.

If you don't have the spare dollar or time for lessons, then just go on YouTube and type in 'How to dance in a club' There are some spoof ones but if you persevere you will find some that are very good, and you can learn for free. Teach yourself from the comfort of your own bedroom; just make sure you close the curtains so the neighbours don't see.

Once you have a few basic moves in your arsenal and feel more confident then you will notice that as long as you look like you're enjoying yourself then you will get an increased amount of female attention. This is because they realise that you're not just there grinding on girls and checking them out. You're there because you're having fun and because you want to be. It's important to lose your inhibitions and become relaxed about it because this makes you look more comfortable with yourself and makes you more attractive.

Remember social proof and how others perceive you is as important on the dance floor as it is in any other part of the club. Women find men attractive who attract other females. When women are seen dancing near you and giving you IOIs then automatically you become more attractive to all the other females, making it much easier for you. A lot of guys worry about starting dancing with a girl, and don't know the best way to get her attention, but if you create social proof on the dance floor then women will already have noticed you and you can take it to the next stage.

Look at the girl you want and let her know you're interested. This could be done by pointing at her, sticking your tongue out at her; anything as long as it's absolutely clear that you mean her and not one of her friends. Now smile warmly and hold out your hand for her to take. She will be happy to dance with you because you're a high value man who's the centre of attention, and she'd rather be seen with you than some creep who's just nodding his head to the beat at the bar.

You're doing well so far. You're probably one of the only guys who's not just grabbing women from behind and grinding on them. Now the worst thing you can do at this stage is just to get in close and personal, grab her by the waist and try and force a kiss on her. If she wants a kiss right away then it will be obvious and go for it, but if not then keep dancing and having fun like you have been doing. Mix up dancing close to her with pushing her away and keeping a small distance between you. Repeating this will make her more comfortable because she won't think that you just want to get close to kiss her, she'll get the impression you're enjoying dancing with her. When you dance close to her after pushing her away it will remind her that you are attracted to her but you're not coming on too strong or forward.

When you decide you want to close you should decrease the time you push her away and increase the time you're dancing closer to her making the dance more sexual and intimate. Pull in close, tilt your head and if she looks comfortable then go for it. If you know the music you can time it for when the song cuts out or for a section that you can't really dance to. After the kiss say 'Let's go and sit down' or 'Let's go and get a drink' and you can go from there.

As I said earlier, even the guys who can dance don't know how to capitalise upon it, build social proof and get girls to dance with them. They usually skulk around in their packs staring at girls and if they're drunk enough they might try grinding on some until they get rejected or slapped. The more they do this the lower their value becomes.

If you follow these steps then you'll have fun, add a new dimension to your game and increase your chances of picking up.

Neg theory (Negative theory)

The fundamental theory behind the 'neg' is that it's the kind of comment you would use if you weren't interested in a girl. A light, borderline 'Insult' that shouldn't realistically cause offence especially if it's delivered in a playful, cheeky manner.

An example could be *'Nice outfit, I've seen about three girls tonight with that same thing on'* or *'Nice nails, are they real?'*

Most guys would never dare say this because they'd be too scared of offending the woman and thusly ruining their chances of sex. If you use a neg it acts as a disqualifier and simply gives the woman the impression you're not interested. This is good at the start of an interaction when the bitch shield (See Bitch shields) has the potential to be fully operational. You're breaking the frame of just being another guy who's chatting her up, showing that she doesn't intimidate you and you won't put her on a pedestal just because she's an attractive woman.

The better looking the woman, the more frequently you should use negs on her. Very attractive women, 9s and 10s are used to being hit on all the time and are used to having men fawn over them at every opportunity. If you neg a high quality woman then she won't have a clue what's going on and she'll think 'Why isn't he chatting me up and complimenting me like everyone else?' and she will seek your approval and try and prove herself to you. The bitch shield comes down and you can proceed as normal.

Some other examples of negs are.

'Your nose moves when you speak, aww that's nice'

'Nice hairstyle, is that real or is it a wig?'

'You're so cute just like a little girl, shouldn't you be out skipping or something?'

'I like your belt. My little sister wore one like that to her school disco last week.'

You can find many other ones with a quick internet search, or feel free to invent your own. You can see that they're mildly insulting at worst and as long as they're delivered playfully with a smile you shouldn't upset the target unless she's really uptight.

You can still neg and not be insulting at all for example.

'It's a shame you're a blond because I'm only dating brunettes at the moment'

'You're 5'4? I only date girls over 5'6 at the moment'

These are still negs but are acting more to disqualify and give the impression you aren't hitting on them.

If the girl is a 7 or below then you should be very careful about using negs. Don't use anything that cuts too close to the bone because the less attractive a girl is, the lower her self-esteem, so you might just plain upset her which isn't the aim. This isn't to say that some attractive women don't have low self-esteem. Use your common sense and if a girl reacts badly to a neg then compliment her on another aspect of her appearance such as her bag or jewellery.

Fake time constraint

Imagine you're a hot woman who gets hit on all the time. The first thing you might think if a guy comes over is 'What does he want?' and 'How long's he going to be here for?' The fake time constraint is something you might say which gives the impression that you can't stay for long. If the target doesn't think you're going to hang around then she'll be more receptive to your opener.

If you say something like *'I need a quick female opinion but I only have a minute because my friend's waiting for me at the bar'* Then she'll probably talk to you because she realises a minute isn't a long investment and you're not going to be hanging round all night. You can then build rapport and as things progress she'll forget you said you only had a minute.

HAVING A WINGMAN...OR FLYING SOLO?

Having a good wingman is useful, but never under-estimate the power of flying solo.

Having a wingman

Having a decent wingman on a night out is an invaluable tool. If you really want to get more women then you need to stop going out with AFCS and go out with like minded guys who have at least some skill and want to improve like yourself.

In this section I'm going to talk about why a good wingman is so useful and how you can help each other out.

1: If your wing is talking to a nice girl but she has an ugly friend then make the sacrifice and speak to the friend. You don't have to sleep with her or even be interested in her; you just have to keep her occupied whilst your friend talks to the cute girl. If you don't engage the friend then she might get bored and feel left out and drag the cute friend away. I know from experience that even if a girl likes you, she's always going to be more loyal to long term friends than a guy she's only just met, no matter how tight your game is.

2: Your wing should always be introducing you to hot women. He has his own needs but he appreciates your needs and understands that you will do the same thing for him. You can trust him to open sets of good looking women and know that he's on your side. With him you will find it easier to have more and better quality interactions.

3: Big up your wing. Tell the girls what a great guy he is. How caring, thoughtful or interesting he is. It doesn't matter if it's true or not just make out that it's an absolute pleasure being his friend. Don't mention anything about his wealth if he has money, many women find boasting about this a turn off.

4: Protect your wing from the dreaded AMOG. If you sense the idiot is about to try and interfere or cockblock then make sure you deal with him swiftly (See dealing with AMOGs)

5: If your wing likes a girl he's speaking to then don't hit on her as well. There shouldn't be any conflict between you. Even if she shows interest in you, you should redirect the attention back to your wing. The only exception would be if she was your absolute dream girl then I'm sure he'd understand.

6: Don't go around in groups bigger than two or three as an absolute maximum. Packs of guys are intimidating and it just works best with two. It's hard to involve more than that in an interaction as well as gaming the targets.

Flying solo?

If you're new to the community you might find the concept of going clubbing alone as alien and weird. This is a natural supposition based upon what the constraints of society would have you believe. Many PUAs do go out alone if they need to. Maybe their friends are busy, or maybe they want to try a club that no one else wants to go to? One option would be to stay home; the other would be to go alone.

Clubbing alone is not as daunting and scary a proposition as you would think. I've been out alone many times before and have had great results. You might think it's sad or desperate, or worry about what people will think of you, and what to say if someone asks where your friends are. Trust me, no one is watching you or wondering why you're alone if it looks like you're having a good time. If anyone asks, your friend is at the bar, in the toilet, outside smoking, has taken a girl home, it really doesn't matter. People are far too drunk or preoccupied with themselves to worry about you and what you're doing. Especially at a larger venue.

If you are very bold you could just admit you're out alone looking to meet new friends. Some people might respect you for it. I would, going out of your natural comfort zone, not every guy has the balls to do it, but if you do you're going to be meeting more girls because you can go out whenever you feel like it and not because it fits in with your mate's diary.

If you decide to go out alone and are nervous and anxious, try not to get too drunk to calm yourself. Instead try a simple psychological technique. Imagine your friend is at the club with you, but he's at the bar or in the toilet. Keep repeating it to yourself if any doubt pervades your psyche. This way you will at some level convince yourself that he actually is there, and this can help you relax and enjoy the night as you would normally.

PROBLEMS IN THE BATTLEFIELD AND HOW TO OVERCOME THEM

Sometimes when you're out in the field you can be faced with certain problems and obstacles. I attempt to dissect the most likely ones you will face, and ensure you can overcome them with ease.

Dealing with the bitch shield

The 'Bitch Shield' is a negative and aggressive, unfriendly persona that a girl adopts on a night out. This does not necessarily mean she is a bitch it's just an act she puts on for three main reasons.

1: Girls like to give guys the shit test, weed out the alpha males from the losers. Putdowns and perceived aggressive behaviour is simply a test. The woman will gauge your responses and if you can withstand the barrage of negativity with humility and composure then you're worthy of her time and respect. A woman can't find a man attractive she doesn't respect.

2: Unlike the average man even the average woman gets hit on a hell of a lot. Next time you're out just watch the number of pests you see going up to women, trying to grab them, drunkenly talk to them and generally creep them out. Many girls' defences are up because they are tired of creepy men bothering them. They don't know you are a cool, attractive guy the shield just comes up automatically and doesn't discriminate.

3: She simply might have had a bad day. Her boyfriend might have dumped her, she might have seen a girl with the same outfit on, she might have been told off by her boss at work. Girls are more emotional than guys so she could simply be angry and hung up about an external factor which manifests into her being unpleasant to any man who approaches her.

If a girl is rude or snobby to you straight away then you should 'Kill her with kindness' and comment on the way she's acting in a positive manner. For example if you ask her a question and she's hostile and rudely demands why you're talking to her, you could retort by saying that you thought she looked like a woman of class and intelligence so you wanted her opinion. If she then accuses you of trying to chat her up you could say that you like her straight forward and honest nature and that not many girls have that. You aren't complimenting her and being obsequious, you're just validating her.

The psychology behind this positive validation is that you are not reacting to her hostile attitude, you're showing you're an alpha male not letting it put you off your stride and confidently putting yourself in control of the conversational frame. To disrupt the negative pattern you need to act the opposite way that she would expect and surprise her. She will soon realise you are immune to her line of intimidation and you should be able to proceed as normal.

Under no circumstances should you stoop to her level of negativity and become hostile and rude to her in response. For a start remaining composed will tell her the shield isn't working and make her more likely to act normal, and secondly getting angry with her will put you in a bad mood and create negative energy which could effect you psychologically the rest of the night.

A lot of men will see a woman and think they are automatically unfriendly and will be unreceptive, but don't let this stop you approaching them, if you do this you are neglecting yourself of the chance of meeting a nice girl.

Dealing with rude responses

This is different from a simple bitch shield. I mean you approach a girl and she's extremely rude and aggressive, or she completely blanks you. You're instinctive reaction might be to be abusive back to her and give her a taste of her own medicine but this is not the right path to take. I suppose every woman has a right not to want to talk to you, for whatever reason and there's nothing you can do about it. The best thing you can do is either walk away or make a biting sarcastic remark.

Even if you're the greatest guy in the world this may happen to you but remember this is no reflection upon yourself, she obviously has some inner turmoil and issues she needs to deal with. The worst thing you can do is react and let it get you down. If you let her get into your psyche then it could put you in a bad mood and create negative energy which any future girls you talk to that night will be able to pick up on. Just dust yourself down, next set soldier. Forget the bad interactions and remember the good ones.

Dealing with AMOGs

We all hate the AMOG (Alpha male of group) And we all hate being AMOGed which is when you're in a set and a guy, could be a male friend or a stranger interjects and tries to belittle you or steal the girl away. This process is known as cock blocking and can be a source of immense frustration and annoyance if you don't know how to deal with him. If the AMOG is a male friend of the target then he may like her himself so he'll do everything he can to ruin it for you. In an ideal world if a guy's running game then you should just leave him to it, unwritten rule of the game, but unfortunately these pillocks exist. There are certain measures you can take to reduce the impact he can have.

Ignore him if he intervenes until he gets bored and goes away.

Position yourself so your back is turned away from him blocking him out.

If he's wearing a tight t-shirt say 'Look how muscley he is he looks like Arnold Schwarzenegger in his prime'

If he says something negative about your clothes like they're cheap say 'That's right Primark's finest baby. I wish I could afford to shop where you do' Lines like this can make him lose his composure and screw up his chances with the girl.

Put your arm round him or backslap him to give you the physical edge. If he tries to high-five you or shake hands then ignore it or shake with your hand on top facing downwards and hold it there putting you in the power position.

Basically be playful with him, not aggressive and don't respond to his childish nature and games. If you mock him, don't react to his crap and remain composed then he should realise he looks stupid and bugger off.

If you have a wing with you signal for him to intervene. I always go over and ask the AMOG if he's seen the footy and talk any old crap.

Dealing with the males of a set

A male in a set is not the same as an AMOG. He could be a decent lad you just need to follow a few steps if it's a mixed set. Open him first, be really friendly, compliment him and make him feel good about himself. Once he likes you ask him how he knows the girls. This is good because you can find out if he's with any of them, and if he isn't you can start speaking to the girls. They're more likely to be responsive if they think you're mates with him.

What to do if she says she has a boyfriend

If she says she has a boyfriend then this might not necessarily be true so don't eject as soon as she mentions it. Some girls say they have a boyfriend for several reasons.

Like with the bitch shield, the psychology is that this is a shit test, to weed out the guys who don't know how to attract them. Might sound stupid but some girls do this.

To get rid of a guy she has no interest in and isn't attracted to.

To make them feel more desirable and confident.

They are unsure about meeting a stranger in a club and are not used to being hit on so they say this because they're nervous.

She actually does have a boyfriend!

The first time she mentions a boyfriend ignore it, don't even acknowledge she said it and continue the conversation as normal. Don't let her see that the revelation has affected you in the slightest. This shows that she can't intimidate you and that you're used to talking to women.

If she genuinely does have a boyfriend then she will mention him again. If she keeps on talking about him then personally I would politely eject because I'd get the impression she was serious about him and he wasn't just a guy she was casually seeing. If you want to proceed and don't feel bad about picking up a girl who is already taken then feel free to do so.

Here are a few examples of what I sometimes say when a girl mentions a boyfriend

Me: Cool, it's always good to have two boyfriends. One for Monday to Friday and one for the weekends.

Me: That's what my ex girlfriend said when we first met.

Me: Great he can make us breakfast in bed.

Me: Does he treat you well? I wouldn't.

Or as I said you could just ignore it and continue as normal.

An attractive woman is likely to have at least one man in her life that plays the 'boyfriend' role. She is of high value and will always have options when it comes to men, so even if she doesn't have a boyfriend per se its likely there'll be someone she's dating. As long as she doesn't keep mentioning him just slow things down and proceed as normal because these girls can be seduced just like any other woman.

DEALING WITH LAST MINUTE RESISTANCE (LMR)

Although this part doesn't pertain to the club or bar I still think it is important including it. After all the hard work and effort you've put in attracting a woman, I'm not going to risk letting anything ruin it for you by not mentioning last minute resistance (LMR). LMR is when you bring a girl home and she rejects your sexual advances. You run good game all night, build attraction, and are all over each other in the club. She suggests going back to yours and you think nature is going to take its course when you get the red light. This can be a source of massive frustration if you don't know what you're doing. It happens to a lot of guys believe me. but it's usually manageable if you take the right steps.

Most AFCs would react to rejection by getting angry, frustrated, begging, looking like a needy, desperate idiot or simply giving up. If you do all these things then you will turn her off, and if you push too hard you'll ruin all the attraction and the connection you've spent all night building.

Once you've ruined these things then you've screwed it up. I know it can be a little demoralising but just keep your composure and remember what I'm about to impart.

You have to distinguish between a woman that doesn't want sex and a woman that has LMR. Take your time during foreplay. I know you might want to rush it before she changes her mind, but it's best if you continue building chemistry and turning her on. If you turn her on past the point of no return then her horny animalistic urges will overcome her logical internal objections e.g. she doesn't know you well enough, she's not a slut.

If she objects during foreplay and says something like 'I don't think we should be doing this' then say that you agree and that she is taking advantage of you, hereby reframing the situation so it looks like she's the one seducing you. You can also slow down the foreplay and start talking, making the situation more comfortable. When she's a little bit more relaxed try again. You just need to act casual when she shows resistance. This demonstrates you aren't needy or desperate and makes her feel more at ease.

As a last resort you can use a tactic known in the community as a 'Freeze-out' This is where you control the frame by turning the lights on, checking your Facebook or going to the fridge to get a Coke etc. You deliberately sabotage the sexy and seductive atmosphere and ruin the state you've built. Women like pleasant sensations, and she won't like you taking this away from her. As a result, if you go back to her then she should be more receptive to your overtures.

Sometimes girls say no just as a token gesture to show that they aren't easy, and it requires a bit more work before they have sex with you. If she says no verbally but has no objections to you proceeding physically, then you can continue.

If you can tell she just doesn't want sex then you just have to accept it. I know it's annoying but it's just one of those things.

Most LMR can be blasted. In my experience many girls put up at least some, so don't be surprised, but know how to respond to it.

TEXT GAME: HOW TO CAPITALISE AND MAKE SURE YOU GET DATES AND SEX FROM THE GIRLS YOU NUMBER CLOSE

Again I know this section doesn't pertain to the club or bar per se, but I've decided that I would be doing you guys a disservice if I didn't include a simple texting guide. My motives are the same as for doing the LMR section, I don't want you go out and have some top quality interactions with some nice women, and then when it comes to contacting them afterwards your text game is all wrong. I'm not prepared to let that happen after the distance a lot of you may have come so far on your personal journey.

Before I got involved in the community my text game was completely dismal and pathetic. I'd often text girls in the old days, but they'd soon lose interest and stop replying to me before I could get them to meet me. I had some dates and sex from girls I number closed on nights out, but it was a low proportion of the numbers I managed to get. As I learnt more and more I discovered that texting women was a different dynamic to texting friends and people you've known for years. This might seem obvious but it wasn't to me, and I want to make sure you don't make the same mistakes. I experimented and tried out new texting techniques until I discovered ways that made it far easier for me to meet up with a girl after getting her number on a night out. If a girl gives me her number now then I'm pretty confident that in most circumstances I can get her to agree to meet me.

First of all we need to understand the reasons why men sometimes have trouble meeting up with women after they've got her number.

1: Time constraints. Most attractive women have many friends and men who are chasing them and they will get more invites to parties, social events etc than an average looking girl might. This means it's harder to get her attention and agree to a date when you have to contend with all these other external factors.

2: Motive. She might think what do you want? Do you expect sex?

3: Safety. She doesn't really know you and you don't have friends in common. Can she trust you?

4: General timing. You know what women are like, she might just be in a bad mood or busy when you text, or she's genuinely scatterbrained and doesn't know what she wants. It's a woman's prerogative to act unpredictably.

5: Fear of it being awkward. You got on well in the bar amongst friends. But in sobriety when it's just you two won't it be awkward or weird?

6: She has a boyfriend. She was attracted to you but she's decided she can't cheat on him, and she wants to stay with him.

7: Guy in the club. You had fun together but she sobers up and the next day she just thinks of you as the guy in the club.

The process of a girl not responding to your messages is known as 'Flaking' if she doesn't reply she 'Flaked' and she is a 'Flake'. This can be very annoying but thankfully there are some measures you can take to reduce the chances of this happening to you. You need to pay special attention to developing rapport. I know this can be hard in a club sometimes but if you really like her and want to see her again then it's imperative you build a deep connection. If you make this connection then she will remember you, and want to see you again because you're more than just the guy she had a laugh with at the club. If you can get her to open her heart and soul to you, and get to that place in her psyche that not many do, then it's increasingly likely that she'll want to see you again.

I'm not saying this deep connection is the only way to guarantee seeing her again I just mean it gives you the best odds. For example I've got girls numbers when drunk before, ran some pretty crappy game then text them and slept with them the next day. If a girl is attracted to you and is a bit of a slut then this can happen but it's generally far less likely, so it's best to develop the deep connection.

Texting and not calling is definitely the best method to reinitiate contact. It's non committal and casual. Sometimes people don't answer their phones for many reasons; They're in public, they're at work etc. Texts are more unobtrusive. There's no pressure on her to have an immediate conversation with you. She can message you back at her own pace, when she feels like it. It's a low-investment, low-risk type of communication which you should always begin with.

Women love texting and your messages will remind her of the reason she was attracted to you in the first place. Now ignore what you might have heard about waiting a few days to contact her. The flawed logic behind this is that if you wait and 'play it cool' it shows you aren't overly keen or desperate. But what if she likes you and is waiting for you to message? You might not be the only guy texting her so crack on! And most importantly the longer you leave it, the more likely it is that the attraction she felt will dissipate and you'll lose that amazing connection you built time and effort creating. This is why you should text her the next day. I always do it after 6pm simply because if she goes to uni or works it's more likely she'll have finished and will be chilling at this time so I can get her attention easier. If you know she has the next day off then I'd still leave it to later afternoon rather than as soon as you get up to avoid looking too keen.

Your first text is very important and you have to do your utmost to get her to respond. The best way to do this is to reference something funny that you shared with her when you met. If you do this it will trigger the happy memories of the conversation. For example if you met a girl called Fiona and she was a nurse at a care home and told you an old man moved in who she'd befriended then you could say.

'Hey Fiona, nice to meet you last night. Hope that old man turns out to be really rich so he can buy you loads of nice things and take you on holiday :)'

Or if you met a girl called Emma and given her the pet name 'Little Emma' and used kino to tease her about her cold hands you could say.

'Hey little Emma, nice to meet you last night. Hope you've managed to warm your hands up a bit today :)'

Those are just a few examples I have used in the past but you can improvise and invent your own based upon your own interactions.

Once she's replied then you've instigated text game. Remember these points before you proceed.

1: Match her texting style. If you text her and she replies in half an hour then text her back in half an hour or a slightly longer time. If she sends you short messages then you do the same thing back to her. The reason is that if you write back straight away then at some level it communicates a needy, unattractive quality whereby you're sitting there phone in hand staring at the screen waiting for her response. It shows you have nothing better to do or any other plans. Even if you don't you need to give the impression you do. You should match her short messages if she starts doing them because writing long ones trying to stimulate a conversation says at that moment you really want to talk to her more than she wants to talk to you. Again a very needy, unattractive thing that you should avoid.

2: Avoid boring messages. Avoid boring subjects and initially keep it light and positive. Don't talk about your job or how cleaning your room is going. Instead talk about funny, out of the ordinary things that will grab her attention. For example you saw a man walking a cat down the street on a lead and it was wearing a jacket, or you saw a man doing crazy dancing in the city centre, he wasn't busking but he made more money than any musician you've ever seen. Men who don't know text game usually just write mundane, dull things and this puts them in the category of all the other boring guys who don't know how to create interest via texts.

3: Use statements not questions. Don't just put 'how are you? , 'What are you up to?' etc. Most men who don't have text game ask loads of questions. You should be making interesting conversation that makes her want to invest.

4: Go for the meet. When you've built a bit of comfort you should consider trying to arrange a meet. Don't be too forceful. If she seems really keen then ask her to meet you outright. If she's a bit more detached and you get the impression she might not be up for a one on one then say something like.

'Hey Katy, a couple of friends and I are going to this new bar on Friday night, do you fancy it?'

'Hey Lisa a few of us are going to see this band at the student union on Saturday you should come?'

This gives the impression you won't be alone. You could even suggest she brings her friends. She might be a bit shy so wouldn't be up for a one on one, but as part of a group she'd be more comfortable and you could run your usual game.

5: Know when to quit. I don't like to be negative but you may feel you're not getting anywhere; she's being vague and won't commit to anything. Most guys respond to this by writing longer messages and texting more frequently. Trying too hard will just look needy and desperate and won't do you any favours. Once you get the feeling things are going wrong it's practically impossible to build the attraction again without actually seeing her again in person. It's a bitter pill to swallow, but learn to stop texting. Don't ask her what you did wrong or how you messed up. You maybe desperate to know and maybe you have a right to, but remember you can't force it.

If you follow these steps then it should dramatically improve your chances of getting girls to text you back and ultimately agreeing to a meet.

ALTERNATIVE WAYS TO GAME

Everything you have learnt in this book is a product of my own experience and the guidance and advice from the very best in the pick-up community. It has taught you how to open, transition to mid-game and hopefully close. It has shown you how to deal with problems you might encounter and how to generally get better results. This is the best way for you to improve your chances with women in the club and bar environment.

However...

What I'm about to say, you won't find in any other PUA book because it goes against the very fibre of what the community believes in. I thought I would involve this because other PUA books consider their words to be sacrosanct, and that a deviation from these techniques could only result in failure.

I just wanted to remind you all that you can eschew said techniques and still obtain some level of success especially at a club from maybe 1am onwards. No other PUA would publicly admit this because it undermines the community, but if you're just looking to pull then remember you could do far worse that simply open, open, open like a madman.

Usually it's easiest to extract women from clubs between 1am and 2.30am. This is because no one wants to go straight to the club and then just leave, if you're a woman anyway. Girls want to spend time with their friends and have a few drinks, loosen up a little. After 1am everyone is usually suitably lubricated with drink, so if you want to cut straight to the chase, but don't mind a bigger likelihood of rejection then I would suggest just speaking to as many women as possible, simplify and condense your routines and just try and ascertain if they're on the pull as well.

If you're in a large club and do a succession of openers and are rejected, then women in the other parts of the club will probably not have seen it, so you can still talk to them without them realising you have been haphazardly patrolling the club opening set after set. You don't really build much of a connection if you play the numbers game, but as I said if you just want to pull and don't mind the bigger chance of rejection then go for it. You have to have a short term memory for this. You're usually avoiding the comfort and connection building stages and just using quick fire direct routines. If you throw enough mud then eventually some should stick because it's a fact that some women will simply be out to pull. If she's had a few drinks and she finds you physically attractive then success will be less dependent on you developing a real 'connection'. Also the quality of women you will be able to attract will be lower than if you used the techniques from the book simply because average woman are more plentiful and have lower standards then high-value women. They might not necessarily be as desirable as you wish, but if you're just looking for quick a one-night stand then go for it.

I'm not advocating taking advantage of drunken women I just wanted to make you aware that you shouldn't be afraid or ashamed to play the numbers game just because of the parameters of what the PUA community says. I don't do this personally but several of my friends do, it's quite hit-and-miss but they get some level of success. If you just want a one night stand then there's nothing wrong taking this path. Just don't forget if it was late on and she was drunk when you met then in the morning she might have buyer's remorse. This means as a result of the intoxication and the fact that you bypassed building an emotional connection, she regrets what she did. You have to make sure you don't take this personally and I would learn to accept it because if you skip the emotional connection and just escalate at the first opportunity, then she probably won't feel close enough to you to want to see you again. This isn't a rule. Most of my mates who go by this technique don't see their conquests again, occasionally the girl turns into a casual partner, but very rarely a serious relationship. If you can handle the emotional detachment of interactions of this nature then go for it but if you want something a little deeper from a girl then I would concentrate on the connection building.

As I said you'll have to develop quite a thick skin for this because you'll be rejected more going this direct. If you don't mind then do it. If you live in a bigger city then it's better because there are usually lots of different clubs open every night of the week, so people probably won't notice the fact that you're doing this so regularly. If you live in a small town and everyone goes to the same small club then you should be aware of the impact on your social proof and value, because a venue of this size in a small town could be frequented with the same people, and you don't want to build a reputation with the local girls as a womanising player.

IN CONCLUSION

Well that was good. I hope you've found this helpful and interesting, and hope it contains information you can incorporate into your nights out to get some decent results.

I realise there's a lot to take in but remember one step at a time. Rome wasn't built in a day. It will take a while to master every aspect and nuance but patience, commitment and the will to improve and better yourself is key. You'll notice yourself improving the more and more you learn and internalise, but don't forget that the real battle is won on the field. You must remember to go out and actually practice. The quicker and more often you go out, the quicker you will start getting better and yielding success.

When I see men at clubs and bars the majority do the same old tired things I have told you to avoid. They keep repeatedly doing them hoping for different results which is the definition of insanity according to Einstein. Einstein was a significantly more intelligent person than I am, or ever will be, but he's not entirely correct in this instance. The same old tired routines on a long time scale might get you some sporadic luck from a drunk and ugly girl, but if you want impressive results with attractive women then please heed my advice.

Go out with your wingman or alone and don't forget to have fun. Don't forget not to drink too much, alcohol can improve your confidence but can also slow you down mentally when you need to be on the ball.

Even though you're desperate to show off your new found knowledge and skills just remember that picking up women isn't the be-all and end-all. You have your friends, your job, school, university, the gym, sports etc. It's important to remember that you have these other things in your life too. It's easy to become engrossed in theory and going out putting new techniques into practice, but it's best to retain a balanced lifestyle. Work on your pick up skills but also do something physical, intellectual and social with your time each day as well. This will help you be at your physical and mental peak in everyday life which will help with your pick up anyway.

The things I've talked about in this book are exactly the things the average guy is NOT doing. So having come this far has put you at an advantage already because you know the pitfalls and common mistakes and know how to avoid them. The average guy does not know how to avoid them so you have the edge over 95% of men.

There are no boundaries to what you can achieve and how far you can get in the game. If you're committed and learn then there's no reason why you can't become just as good as any of the world famous PUGs (Pick up gurus) such as Neil Strauss and Mystery. There were times in their lives when they were beginners and lacked experience, and I'm sure they aren't anymore charming, funny or good-looking than you are.

I want to share it with you and whatever you're looking for; a one night stand, a casual relationship or a girlfriend, then I hope this book will help you achieve your targets.

If you like what you've read then please don't forget to post a review for me.

Thanks and good luck gentlemen.

Made in the USA
Las Vegas, NV
23 January 2022

42158283R00046